High on Cloud Joyous

High on Cloud Joyous

and Other Poems

Elvina Schullere

Rivertowns
BOOKS

Printed in the United States of America

ISBN-13: 978-0-9790080-4-7
ISBN-10: 0-9790080-4-2

LCCN Imprint Name: Rivertowns Books

Rivertowns Books are available online from Amazon as well as from bookstores and other retailers. Queries and other correspondence may be addressed to:

Rivertowns Books
240 Locust Lane
Irvington NY 10533
Email: info@rivertownsbooks.com

CONTENTS

AUTHOR'S NOTE

Each of these poems was born after a mental lightning blast in reaction to an observation, a happening, an angry thought, an experience, or an emotion, wherever I happened to be—on sea or land, in an automobile, on foot or on bicycle, on a flight or upon awakening.

Thank you for reading these poems--I hope you enjoy them.

Elvina Denise Whittaker-Schullere

SOLITUDE

I say it's no good
As I sit and worry
In my hand a book
Yet the pages are empty.

My troubles are many
And love there's none;
A friend there isn't any
And my ambition's all gone.

Music is no longer soothing
My heart is ready to break
Painting too seems boring
I wonder what's my fate.

Even a job I can't fin
So I sit and weep.
You ask what's on my mind?
I had better go to sleep.

April 13, 1950

ODE TO KAREN

Smoother than the plushest velvet is my little
baby's skin.
Softer than a summer breeze is my little one's hair.

More gentle than a sea breeze on a summer night
is my baby's touch,
And her dark eyes dance like snow flake in the
sky.

May, 1963

TO KAREN (1)

Aged four or five

Who is my little girl? A tomboy
With a cute and awkward gait.
She climbs on banks and writes on walls.
She loves to go swimming and flir with big boys.
She loves books and rubber bands,
Doesn't care much for toys.
She loves to cook and say "No!"
My little girl, her dark eyes like rare gems
And laughter like a nightingale's song.
She loves to dance and run, and say
"Hello" and "Goodbye" to everyone.

1967

IN MEMORY OF DR. MARTIN LUTHER KING, JR.

Death! Death! Oh, what are you?
Some ugly thing or something of beauty?
Something cruel or something happy?
Ah! No.
A little girl, no Dad to kiss good night.
A wife no longer shares her bed, her secrets, her
joy, her sadness.
Oh, you selfis fiend—n longer will he see the
stars at night
Or budding blossoms in the spring
Or the rising of a silvery white snowy bed
Or the whispering frothy folds of a summer sea.
No longer will he see Black sad faces
Or hear happy people sing.
So many things he will not see again or hear or
touch or feel.
No marches, walks, no sermons, promises or talks.
No fears, humor, no love, hopes or future.
Ugly death. All cloaked in white.
You disturb, cheat the good, sadden the night.

April, 1968

IN MEMORY OF SENATOR
ROBERT F. KENNEDY

They kiss him one by one
Then turn around and leave him lying there
alone . . .
My heart is pained, my eyes are brimming.
He is alone.
Yet I am puzzled, I do not understand.
'Twas only two score hours ago!
His beauty, laughing charm, his pious greatness,
His million friends about him.
Now he lies alone.
But does he really lie alone?
His brother lies nearby waiting for him.
Once again, he is his brother's keeper.

June, 1968

TO DARIUS

Oh beautiful boy—
He hates to be kissed
He has two dimples
And a lisp.

He has long braids
When will I cut them?
He is so agreeable
With his big brown eyes
And ruddy face.

1970

LOST IN TIME

Yes, Ken, you say your life was interrupted.
But everything is standing still!
Even from where I sit—a solarium, quite
appropriately called—
I can see the river, dark and quiet,
Unruffl   by those moving objects, large and
small;
The forest of trees beneath seem to stand guard for
you, my darling,
Quietly praying, unswaying, as if in reverence for
your suffering
Everyone is beautiful—young and old, rich and
poor.
They reach out to me, a hand, a lift, a smile,
A promised prayer . . . kind deeds and love.
My dearest, you are not alone.
Sincere doctors Di Palma and Schwarz,
A devoted sister, concerned brothers,
A kind-hearted loving boss, your loyal men, your
caring children,
Patient nurses, Odessa, beautiful Odessa,
Cheri, pretty blue eye Cheri, her caring showing in
her eyes,

And Iris caring for you like she had none other to
care for,
Mrs. Booker, Tom and Cantrell, all of them aides
and nurses,
Caring, teasing, loving, caring.
A God who loves you, spared you, and all
inquiring friends,
And Father George who calls your name in holy
remembrance.
You're not alone—and me.

Summer, 1977

THE MIST IS LIFTING

On the grounds of Burke Rehabilitation Hospital

The mist is lifting
And among the buds of yellow
        I look for a beautiful leaf.

But how do you pick a diamond
From a sea of gems?

The day is just awakening.
The odor of pine fill the air.
The sun smiles for a minute.
The birds orchestrate in beautiful melody.

I pause to look behind me
And behold! A beauteous sight:

A winding path that quietly leads
To a gateway of golden yellow
Fallen leaves,

A gateway to everlasting paradise.

Oh! What indelible beauty!

October 27, 1977

THE SNOW IS FALLING

Yesterday from my window
I looked at glass trees,
Glistening like diamonds in the sunlight.

Today the sun swallowed them
And the trees stand naked and bare again,
But tonight, ah tonight,
The snow is falling, falling, falling,
The river merges with the Palisades,
The Palisades with the sky,
Until there is a great grey curtain,
The night becomes still and quiet,
Yet every second a pair of glaring
Lights go crawling by,
As though afraid to disturb the quiet whiteness.

January 20, 1978

TO KAREN (2)

Nothing can replace our loss . . . your loss
But the item lost itself. I do feel
The anguish and sense of helplessness you are
experiencing.
But you must know that life is a series,
A balance of happiness and crisis.
The crisis jolts us from complacency.
We are supposed to grow out of our experiences.
This is by the law of being.
Don't allow this experience to throw your
emotions
Out of perspective. We must learn
To handle crisis and come out stronger.
You would survive as you survived a far greater
loss.
If you can surmount this, then the greatest lesson
Would be self-preservation and control.
This is the law of being—
And another step in your growth to a human
being.

1982

VAN CORTLANDT PARK IN WINTER

Lying, sleeping, resting,
>> It is quiet now.
Looks like a graveyard, mournful and clothed
In white,
Tall bare silhouettes scattered here and there,
>> One man,
>> One dog still intrude upon my
>> solitude.
Soon enough
>> I will shed my cloak to green.
Then will I hear the constant tap, tapping
>> Of feet upon my head?
The thunderous chatter of balls
>> Flying through the air,
>> Thrown with vengeance from a bat,
And cricketers in white garb run back and forth
>> To touch their stakes!

February 17, 1983

TO MARY

My astrologist friend and artist

Your singing stirred me.
        You had something to say
With movements free and from the soul.

You stomped and swayed,
        You bowed, and our hearts sang out.

Black lace and flamin   hair
        And strings aloft.
The chilling rolls of percussion . . .
        Guitar and cittern ranked . . .

And you sang of heroes and heroines.
Then I remembered Sting! Baez! Makeba!
        Yes! All with visions in song . . .

But you did it well,
        Your movements tell
So sweet, so honest . . . from the love
        You did it well.

March, 1987

A PRAYER

For my son Darius Antony on his 32nd year in the universe

Physical, emotional, intellectual growth
Are part of what it means to be human
So that you may evolve to be the best
Human being you can be . . . O Lord I pray:
To see only the good in our fellow brothers and
sisters
And contribute to that good . . . O Lord I pray:
To let God's light be in your heart
So you can listen to others and not
Shout them out . . . O Lord I pray:
To be just, considerate of all, to be understanding
And most of all unselfish . . . O Lord I pray:
To take complete responsibility for your life,
Being, health, and for everything that contributes
To your personal growth . . . O Lord I pray:
To be kind, gentle, loving and giving . . . O Lord I
pray:
Above all else, you must do
What must be done for you . . . O Lord I pray.

1990

REFLECTIONS

Plush green trees, shrubbery and plants of the
summer
Lend to therapeutic healing and calm,
Healing of the human soul and mind.
Alas! This majestic greenery turns to orange, red,
Yellow, brown, and all diffe ent hues.
This, to charge our solar plexus, our internal
environment
Thus preparing humankind and charging our
electric meridians
For the changing of the season—winter.

Having done this course, the beauteous leaves
Loosen their grip with or from their mighty
Wooden frames. Like fallen eagles they carpet the
earth,
Leaving beds of color all around us.

Then like a universal sweep, strong winds
Sweep and chase the fallen leaves into oblivion.
Where did they all disappear?

The inevitable rain from the internal forces
Then beats the dying leaves into the earth

From which they originated, and the cycle
Goes on and on. Amen.

October 31, 1991

HIGH ON CLOUD JOYOUS

High on cloud joyous am I!
Bursting and exhilarated with happiness.
My heart . . . my mind . . . great!
I am beautiful.
I have music, beautiful music—Queen.
Love it! Love it! Love it!
I have my health,
My mother dearest,
My brother dear,
My Karen sweet,
My family devotees,
My life,
My activities,
My voice,
My business,
My friends,
My blessings,
My courage,
My fortitude,
My faith,
My goodness,
My love—
I am great!

I am getting in returns thousandfold. Thank you,
God!
Don't pick up on sadness; not my cup of tea!
I love me.

1992

THE LAST HURRAH

Show oﾢ your snow-white gown!
Let me wed the winter to the spring.
Your snow-white train pedestaled by the bare
brown
Trees and green pine trees.

Cover your bare arms!
I must express my mighty power.
Alas! To make my fina statement
To the universal wretched complacency.

Oh beauteous white wonderland
I am magical . . .
I can grip the branches until I turn
To icicles that glorify my scene.

My path, my soft white carpet.
I can lie for days or harden my face to
Glassy.

Five ten p.m.—the furry green trees all
Huddled together in these mountains
Like soldiers in wet cloaks.

March 20, 1992

STATE OF THE UNIVERSE

So much hate in the universe!
So much bitterness, so much greed, lust and
violence.
But how long? Who's the watchman here?
To whom does one give accountability?

I say a God. Some say no, some say a force.
Are they angry? Have they seen enough?
Yesterday, like a great conspiracy,
The wind, the rain, the sea went mad.

It was considered one in a century.
The sea invading the land, like spoilers invading
and pillaging.
Cars abandoned and floatin   around like toy ships
in a pond.
The raging winds indiscriminately taking the roofs
Of unsuspecting horrifie   inhabitants and
sometimes taking all
Save the boots and the clothes upon their backs.

Frightened children, pets and old citizens
Rescued by divers to shelters safe.

The Hudson River rose to the land, no dividing
walls,
For the angry forces made everything stop to
notice.

The bridges all closed.
The airport runway resembles a sea.
In the shelters people sit as in a wake, to wait, wait
and watch.

Electric power cut oĀ in most places and towns.
I saw the waves beat up a house in angered
repetition,
Until the house collapsed in slow submission,
Seems so cruel, yes.

Yet in times like this, I reflec at the gross
Injustices and cruelty in the cosmos.
Would it ever end?

I count my blessings as I sit here today.
I look at the snow falling, accumulating in the
grayness
And still so heavy winds
On and on and on.

You miss it all.

December 12, 1992

THE AQUEDUCT

Where can you fin a path to pray, to think, to run
or walk and dream?
To hear sounds of birds and rusting trees which
bring memories to life?
The aqueduct.
Where can you fin a dichotomy in your path and
take the one which leads to one seldom trod,
Of awesome, chilling quiet, and thick forest
likened to the Amazon
And trees so tall they kiss each other in the sky?
The aqueduct.
Where can you fin smiles and hellos that make
you want to sing?
And rocks of white or grey, or purple so smooth
you know a beach or river once did shape them?
Or pick berries of white and purple that leave
your finger indelibly stained?
The aqueduct.
Cyclists young and old, small dogs, large dogs and
cats.
Where would you fin a smiling friend to share a
glass or two of needed water icy cold?
And butterflie that cross your path
To see a deer peering at you just beyond?

Where can you fin   a place to run or walk, to be at
peace?
To hear the black crows bellow loudly on a tree
above, warning that someone is below their
terrain?
Where? Where? The aqueduct,
Just beyond here.

July 4, 1993

TO KAREN (3)

The cage door was never locked.
My bird was free to leave its cage.
Now the cage door opens wide, and my little bird
is free to fl ,
Free to fl , fl my little bird . . . Spread your wings
and soar,
Soar to the heights, soar to the mountaintop . . . Yet
take time to stop and peer,
Keeping faith that He is always there, there to
guide, to protect,
To lead you to the right path always.
With wisdom to make the right decision at all
times . . .
And even if you don't, you shall learn from your
mistakes.

You were a great joy to Ken—and a greater joy to
me.
For my fortune was to have a longer experience:
Your concern, your love, your devotion, your
loyalty to me are virtues that must be
commemorated.
Your strength, your work ethic, your courage,

Your confidence your integrity, fairness in
adversity.
Your intelligence, your beauty, your strong sense
of right and wrong,
Your respect for law, your decency, your strong
commitment and dedication
In whatever you undertake are attributes which
can only be ultimately rewarding.

Go with Peace, my child, to new horizons
With all my blessings.

1998

VIEWING A WAR MOVIE

Squadrons—look at them!
They fl like giant birds, in formation,
With masks that enable them to fl at high
altitude.
Young unsuspecting men
Flying into their neighbors' back yards.
Why are young men so obsessed with war?
With killing men they do not know and never
met?
It's all a ludicrous game, while they sing,
"We are little black sheep who have lost our way."

2003

THERE ARE DREAMS

There are dreams
              Passing,
          Memories fleeting
There is a treasure chest.
          I pull one out.
          It dances in my head.
          It brings great joy.
My treasure chest is laden
          With previous gems.
Yet jaded jewels that were buried
          Sometimes show their ugly heads.

February 25, 2004

OBSERVATION

Men are weak, they fall prey often
To woman's vain folly and vanity.

Seduced in the name of love—
Marc Antony and Cleopatra.

What a fool!

October, 2005

LISTEN TO THE SEAGULLS

Listen to the seagulls in the mall.
They transfer the rippling sound
Of the sea waves to this vast concrete bed.

November, 2005

SIGN OF THE TIME

When no one gives a damn about another!
In bright red jackets, a new breed of female,
A new sport, even at fiftee   years of age.
They delight in shooting down
The unassuming winged creatures in flight
Through the glass partition
I see the tall evergreens swaying
In a flirtatiou   dance with another spruce
Standing tall, other trees have already shed their
leaves.
The leaves blow around the ground in wild
despair
Seeking a place to rest.
The concrete walls of the home look dreary
And everything lies abandoned until life emerges
again.
A funeral of sorts, before my eyes, a soul
Who would not see another dawn,
The pall bearers, the security guard and heralds.

December 6, 2006

WHAT IS TIME?

What is time? It rolls, it blows like the wind,
Like planets spinning from outer space.
Can we hold it? Depends on one's perspective.
I am here, in this glossy musical happening
looking in,
Old family, some gone, and we can hold for a
moment
This spinning planet in time.

I see Daddy, Mother,
I see Darius and Karen
And Leland and his young, and Phyllis gone way
back then—
It's gone,
But I did hold time.

I see Sybil now and Ian, Samantha and their
young.
My God! I am looking back, Karen and Darius
Apart now, he with a wife and child now, Franz
and Ren, Atom and Zen, like Darry and Karen
used to be,

Rafael bursting around like shooting stars in the galaxy,
On the floo running wild.

Yes! You can hold time, even if for a moment.

January 11, 2007

LISTEN TO THE CARDINAL'S SOLO

Listen to the cardinal's solo!
Temporarily reigning on the still tall sleeping tree,
Welcoming spring, which shows its face by high
degree only.

It's only March, victorious over the soft
Billowing white matter turning to ice
Which covered half the planet only yesterday,
Submitting to the rain and Fahrenheit.

Showing its familiar face, the grass,
Long buried and discolored from ice.
Buds emerging from the long outstretched
branches of forsythia,
Happy hyacinth pushing through as though in
labor,
Out of the cold dark womb beneath the dirt.

Little white heads like crowns atop short green
blades,
Following in anxious pursuit,
Shedded jackets, barking dogs orchestrate,
The balmy breeze rustling the chimes,

And bright and brilliant sun daring
To show its face at seven in the morn.

Yet it's quiet. Listen! Listen!

March 27, 2007

ON THE SAW MILL BIKE PATH

Last year I stood six feet tall and proud
Bearing my green attire.
One year later I still stand in limbo
Now in drab brown—waiting, waiting.

I look down at my neighbors
In the messy swamps
Miles of green carpet with crowns of glossy yellow
flowers

As though nature planned it, amidst
A pile of fallen trees, broken limbs
And stumps like sawed-oﬀ walruses
Waiting to be bonﬁ ed.

In brown contrast, mounds of brown
Straw that resemble giant nests for birds.

Along the concrete path, the new green
Life of spring covers the ugliness of last year's
unrelished.

Above me, I hear birds.
At a glance, one dances like a peacock for his
mate.

They seem to be singing to each other
Their long beaks motioning like a conductor's
baton.

April 24, 2007

HAPPINESS

Happiness is . . .
     A hot cup of almond milk, with a sprinkle
of nutmeg dancing on the surface.
Happiness is listening to Freddie Mercury sing
"Mama."
Happiness is sitting quietly on a summer day
     On the opened veranda
     Enveloped by blue skies
     And white moving clouds
        And not a sound.

September 2, 2007

ON THE PORCH

An electric lantern type glows above,
A mosquito flirt with my bony arm,
Crickets sing an unmelodious chorus.

In a distance through the thick oak trees
A cluster of red lights across the river in the
Palisades
Blink in one-quarter time.

Always quiet as I sit here under
The bright lantern above my head,
Aware of the sounds of automobiles driving
On the main street below,

Awaiting Princess Alison.
Here she comes!
That rumbling engine, that BMW.

October, 2007

SNOWFALL

Like millions of sparkles, silvered by the
moonlight,
Dancing, dancing, dancing like laughing eyes
Caressing the face like gentle waves on the sand
Then disappearing like the night.

Then alas! Like marshmallow mountains the
pavements grow,
Floating, floating, floating up—then a frozen
wave,
And the trees, the cars their white jewels show
Inviting little robbers, their tiny fingers mould.

But the beauty rare does seldom live forever.
Dying, dying, dying, slowly in a watery grave,
No longer silvered, beauteous, but disappearing
into nothingness,
And again a hard concrete bed doth reappear.

Winter, 2007

ON THE ROYAL CARIBBEAN—
THE EXPLORER AT SEA

Swells that leave white milky tips sprinkle the
surface of the vast Atlantic,
Sailing slowly, sometimes shaky, tossing its
occupants about.
Stand still! Retrieve one's balance, suspending for
a mere second or two.
At times the wind as mighty as Zeus, powerful as
Apollo,
Sounds like bursts from a machine gun.
I gaze and ponder at this miracle, the vast ocean
and wonders below,
The planet—water, trees, earth, fish
The human—blood, veins, organs, skin, bones.

April 7, 2008

THE FORSYTHIA

The forsythia in her blazing glory
Draped in bright, sparkling yellow

Peeping through the curtain-draped
Window in winter maroon.

We dine here on manna sent by God
Through Karen

In this room warm and gracious,
No blinds to hide the morning sun or hazy days
Nor green trees sprouting, springing and glowing
In the summer morn.

Sleeping in the dark dreary winter
Through white peaks of snow and
Naked trees.

April 30, 2008

HURRICANE IN YONKERS

A tapping at my window yesternight
Arrested my attention.
Peering through my front window, alas!
Alarmed at what I beheld.
Whirling white ghostly dragon-like forms
Spitting large hailstones instead of flames
Beating angrily on each window,
Creating a terrifying din.
Then falling to the grassy lawn,
Forming a white carpet of crystal marbles.
Yet this concept of beauty contrasted its path, like
White locust destroying everything in its trail,
Leaving headless begonias, tomato plants, *et al.*
The hosta lying drooped, its lifeless remains,
Its beautifying nectar-fille   tentacles from which
The hummingbird feasted, all whipped away.
Mud slides and gigantic old trees
No longer majestic, but aged overnight.
The June trees now wear brown in mourning
And side-effecte   from the white dragon's jaws,
Lifeless giants lying atop cars at random.
Sad stories related by neighbors and friends.

The clean-up begins.

Heavy wooden bodies put to rest through magical
Machines that turn tree trunks into crumbs.
Cables hanging everywhere from above,
Wires restrung, fences rebuilt, piles of mud
Shoveled from one side of the street to the other.

We count our blessings and move on.

February, 2009

EN ROUTE TO SABEGO

Spewing pus and cancer, disguised as
Hale and wind.

Storm! Storm!

The trees aging before their term.
The sun in anger, grilling from above,
Burning skin like coal and boiled lobster.
Seventy-fiv degrees feel like a hundred plus
degrees.
Your body wrenches and exorcises accumulated
toxins.
We shudder, we groan, we sigh.

Rivers contaminated by uncaring selfis
companies.
Plastic, plastic,
Another creation in the ocean,
In the bellies of turtles, fis and creatures
Of the sea world.
Melting glaciers and little hope for the inhabitants.

Extinction threatens!

Bees are disappearing!
Birds are dropping!

Who is minding the planet?
Who cares? Who is the gatekeeper?
Few care. To what have we come?
Hey! Yo! Supersizing, superdumb.

August 23, 2009

MEDITATION

Sitting here today,
No empty thoughts remiss, but contemplation.
The day crickets sing their song,
Others answer.
I listen!
They pause,
Then blend into my thoughts like a symphony—
   Major, minor scales.

September 4, 2009

YOUR QUIET STRENGTH (FOR ZEN)

Your quiet strength that slept till now
Doth awaken and stirs our souls.
You, now a warrior,
We, the champions
Leading the charge
In prayer, in love and fortitude
We battle!
Mom and Dad,
Grandma and Karen,
Stef, yes, Stef,
Rafael, Darry,
Winnie, Aunt Sybil from Unity,
Uncle Darius and Renée, too,
Nayna prays to Krishna for you,
Rita Gerstle and Joanne to St. Jude.
You show us how to be quiet yet brave.
Oh beauteous child of God,
Oh noble child of the universe,
You show us how to be brave,
To be brave, to be brave.

August 3, 2010

OBSERVATION

Trees bring us joy,
Tall spruce, medium and midget-sized.

So tall they are that they are cut down
In their prime, shortening their life,
Just to be donated to parks and centers
To be adorned with colorful lights and ornaments,
Tinsel of silver, red, or gold—
Sudden death, sudden abandonment!

So-called Christmas spruce too, cut down in their
prime,
Taken to homes poor and wealthy, decorated
In splendor and ritual grand,
Then quickly discarded!

Next stop: Christmas tree graveyard,
Piles and piles of shrouded trees lie
Sadly on the sidewalks,
The jubilance, the joy and peace
They all bring us, so short-lived.

Then there is another row of trees.
They bare no beauty

But wrench joy from the soul.

These trees attract a familiar plague—
Plague of the plastic bags,
Black, beige, white and yellow
They race up and down the street
Scattered here and there
Dancing in the wind, on fences too,
Caught on the cables of parked cars,
On the beach, rolled in with the tide
And in the bellies of the water world.

March 3, 2011

FOR BARBARA

Upon arising I whisper
Barbara, Barbara like a quiet mantra.
I pause atop the stairs.
I recall seeing you through the glass windows at St
      B, walking through very heavy rain in the
      parking lot, carrying something or other.
I recall you walking to your car to return a plant
      your borrowed from the Playhouse to
      decorate the hall for my recital in 2004.
I recall you securing a path to the ladies room at
      the Playhouse during intermission of an
      event.
I recall your quiet, sturdy steps through the halls
      of St B in preparation for one sale or
      another, toting, lifting, caring.
I recall Kimiko's wedding, where I glanced
      sideways as I stood with friends, and you
      glanced from across another space and our
      glances met.
Dearest Barbara, my entire being is with you
      today.

March 14, 2011

TO DARRY

You were born special
A child with promise
A child with special gifts—
A special smile, a musical smile,
A smile of hope and grace,
A genius deep inside you.
Oh genius, awake, awake!

May 28, 2011

SUNDAY

What is Sunday?
Who is Sunday?
     A collection of diffe ent people worldwide.

It is quiet
It is sounds
It is singing
It is church
It is organ
It is cricket
It is peaceful

I remember Sundays back in the colony.

Sunday is silk, organdy, crêpe, and frills,
Sunday school, and the Queen's Park, Savanah.
Sunday is band concert and tram rides around the
Savanah.
Sunday is outings with Daddy, Mother, and Earl
my brother.
Sunday is coconut water vended outside the
Savanah.
Sunday is crab and callaloo, beef and pork stew
with pigeon peas.

Sunday is pound plantain and cassava.
Sunday is coconut ice cream and barbadine.
Sunday in Hawaii same as Italy and as Paris:
People promenading in their Sunday best.

Sunday is quiet, only interrupted by the songs of
birds or rumbling automobiles.
Sunday is like no other day in the week.
Sunday is, Sunday is!

2011

FLORIDA MEDITATION

In Heron's garden
I sit on an upturned plastic container
Permanently standing on a pumpkin-colored brick
path
Among the beds of lavender periwinkle
Umbrellaed by a carambola tree, still young.

A butterfly flutters by, an ant invades my paper,
A young lizard springs from a tall
Blossoming pigeon pea tree to a smaller one.

Beyond, two young girls on skate boards,
One pirouetting in graceful balanced rhythm
While the other struggles to keep up.
The breezes flow through the garden.
A car now interrupts the peaceful silence.

The sky so blue, spotted by large white puffs.
The neighbor's generator begins to moan
And the silence is broken.
I see a beautiful red dwarf rose plant
By the tall lavender periwinkle.

March 18, 2012

I WAIT FOR MAY

Stand behind me,
Master Rafael and Miss Alison.
It's a long time coming.
I wait for the smell of rain and cut grass,
For sprouting buds
                    all yellow,
Tulips, forsythia, and hyacinth though purple and
pink.
From the new leaves bursting to life from the tall
dried trees,
Greener than in August and September
When they are processing change like a praying
mantle.
I wait for May to sing "A May Morning,"
And on the 28th I pay tribute to this special day—
my birthday—
By song and dance and feasting.
May has been kind to me,
Talent, health and unrelenting joyous spirit.
The cardinals sing for me too!
The blue jays!
Even the squirrels do high wire tricks for me,
Cards, calls and kisses all for me.

Even Darry born to me on my day—
                    his also!
I wait for my May,
I wait for May.

May 2, 2012

IN DEERFIELD BEACH, FLORIDA

I lie here on this morn,
No sunny skies today; gray on gray.

I am anchored in my bed as mind
Whispers, *Take a walk.*
But joggers are absent from
The street so still.

There is a hurricane watch!
I fear being swirled oÃ the ground
By the majestic winds.
The tall palms trees sway in rhythm
To the music of the wind.
Other trees pick up the choreograph
In will abandonment.
A single bird swiftly flutter by,
A break from the scorching sun.

Last night the thunderous roar,
Blazing lightning, bringing forth heavy
Sparkling rains and darkness.
Some crept through the door.

The heavy rain beat upon the shrubs and flowers
Beauty, blood-chilling beauty. Elvina was here
To witness it all.

August 5, 2012

EVIL DRESSED IN BLACK

Evil dressed in black.
Black tie and tails.
Black suits, white shirts.
White men in disguise
Corporate garb
Superficia persona,
Medusan brains.
Evil personified
White men, corrupt and greedy.

2010

EARL DARLINGTON WHITTAKER

"I shall pass this way but once; any good that I
can do or any kindness I can show to any human
being; let me do it now. Let me not defer nor
neglect it, for I shall not pass this way again."—
Etienne de Grellet

This is my brother's life.

Philanthropist, engineer,
Uncle, brother,
Son, friend, dancer,
Body builder, calypso lover.

His life enviable, full and interesting.
Origin Woodbrook, Port of Spain, Trinidad.
To U.S., American school, Seward Park High
School.
To England for the Royal Air Force.
He taught Sunday school there, and fed Cadbury
chocolate
To his friends, the Russels,
And helped his fellow airmen out of debt.
Not much money left . . . but he is still giving.

2017

TO FRANZ SCHULLERE, 1953 – 2017

You came into this planet quietly.
I, on the other hand, made a terrible din:
No knowledge of childbearing,
No knowledge of child birthing.
Conceived in Bamberg, Germany—
Hence the name Franz,
Thought up quickly as a name was requested.

Never touched the floor,
Always in white rompers,
Always in Mummy's arms.
An opportunity you seized one day:
We were all outdoors;
You just got up and started walking,
Walking so fast I screamed.

Very high I.Q. was your gift.
Class clown at St. Mary's School.
You abhorred the brothers at Mount St. Michael
Academy.
Brother viewed you as a Panther.
Artistically talented, you drew fists—
Daddy and Mommy were summoned.
You were honored with First Place

In the Catholic Youth Organization contest in our parish,
Third Place in the entire archodiocese.
This piece of art hangs in our main room for all to see.

2017

ACKNOWLEDGEMENTS

Many thanks to Karl Weber, our gracious vestry member at the Church of St. Barnabas in Irvington, New York, who inspired me to ask him to read some of my collection of poems.

To Karen Schullere, my devoted daughter, for her kind attention.

To Sharon De Backer, my friend, who volunteered to type.

To Kumiko Buller, our great and talented artist at St. Barnabas, for permission to use her portrait of me, which formerly hung in the Red Hat restaurant in Irvington, on the cover of this book.

Elvina Denise Whittaker-Schullere

ABOUT THE AUTHOR

Elvina D. W. Schullere was born on May 28, 1929, in Woodbrook, Port-of-Spain, the capital of Trinidad, then a British colony. She attended private schools in Trinidad. In 1948, she moved to New York City with her father, Eustace D. Whittaker, her mother Marguerite, and her brother Earl D.

Based on her school transcripts from Trinidad, Schullere was required to attend high school for two years to receive her academic diploma. She attended Wadleigh High School in Harlem, the firs all-girls' public high school in New York, earning a place in the honor society Arista. She was also selected by Arista to paint a portrait of the school's principal, and another of her art projects was displayed at the Museum of Modern Art (MOMA).

Schullere earned an associate's degree from Seton College in Yonkers and bachelor's, master's, and Ph.D. degrees in clinical nutrition from Donsbach University in California as well as teacher certificatio from Farleigh Dickinson University. She worked as a medical assistant at Mountainview Medical Associates and later worked for five years as a property auditor at Columbia University.

Schullere began singing in Trinidad at age twelve. In New York, she studied with Albert Rhodes and sang with the New York Symphony chorus, conducted by J. Labovitz. She joined the Thomas Music Study Club of the National Association of Negro Musicians and performed at MOMA, Alice Tully Hall, and Symphony Space. At Rutgers Presbyterian Church, she performed in operatic productions produced by Wellington Jones. She now performs with the Canterbury Choir at the Church of St Barnabas in Irvington, New York, directed by Donald Butts.

Schullere has three children: Franz, Darius Antony, and Karen Alison.

ABOUT THE COVER ARTIST

Kumiko Buller, originally from Japan, studied painting at the Art Students League with Harvey Dinnerstein and Ronald Sherr. She is known for her pastel portraits and lives in Ardsley-on-Hudson, New York.

Made in the USA
Las Vegas, NV
02 December 2020

11932942R00049